FROM ATOMS TO ZEROS

A Haylium Picture Book
Jeffery McCain

For Jacob, Henry, and Evelyn

*Special Thanks to
Zena, Racheal, Brittany, and Holly*

We learned about scientists and inventors today. Do you know any?
Of course! I bet I can name one for every letter in the alphabet.

Archibald Alphonso Alexander
built airports, bridges,
and sewer systems.

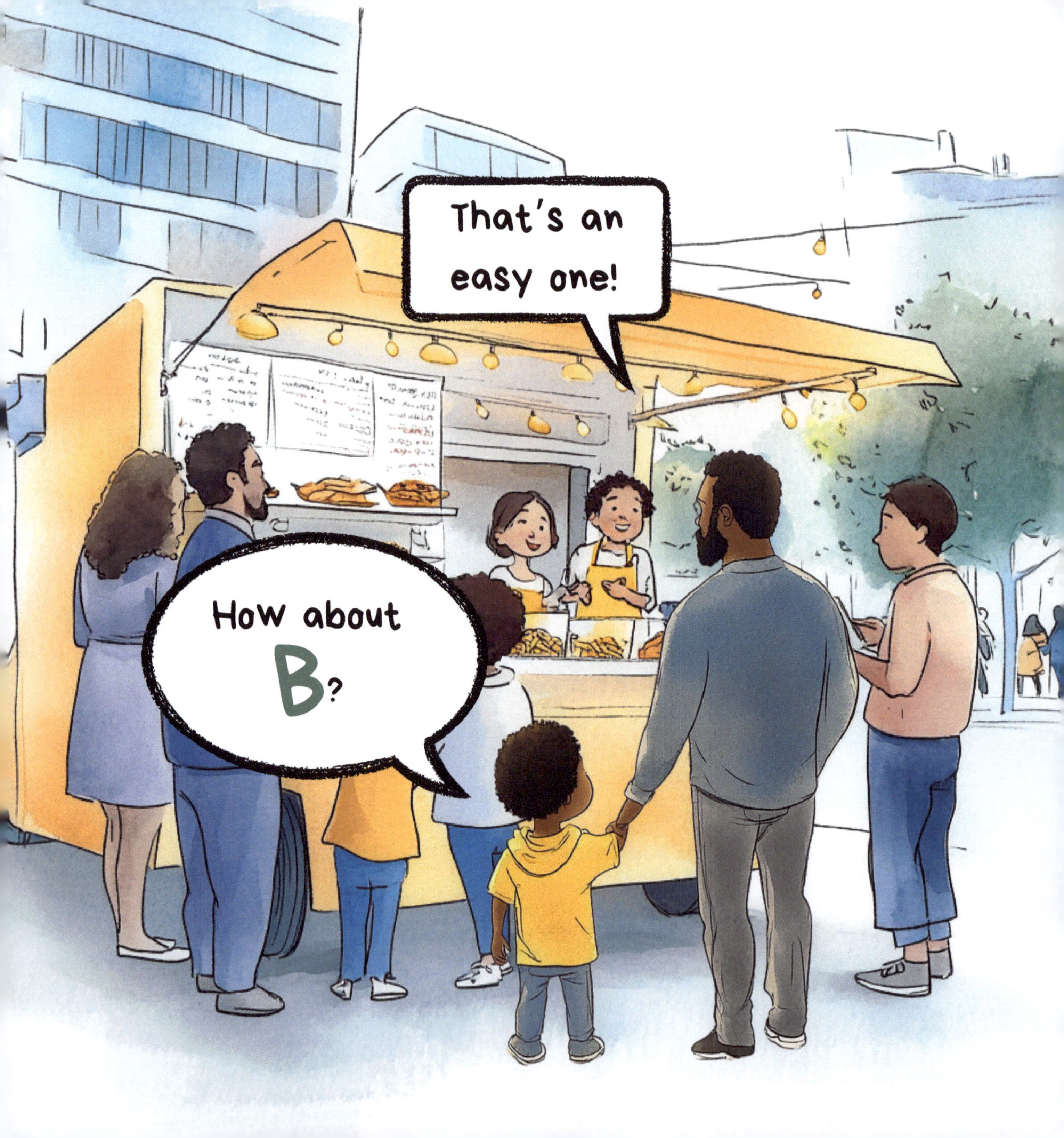
That's an easy one!
How about B?

Bessie Blount Griffin
made a device to help people
without arms feed themselves.

Dr. **C**harles Drew found a way to make
blood last so long it could
be sent across the ocean.

Dr. Neil **D**egrasse Tyson teaches kids about the wonders of space.

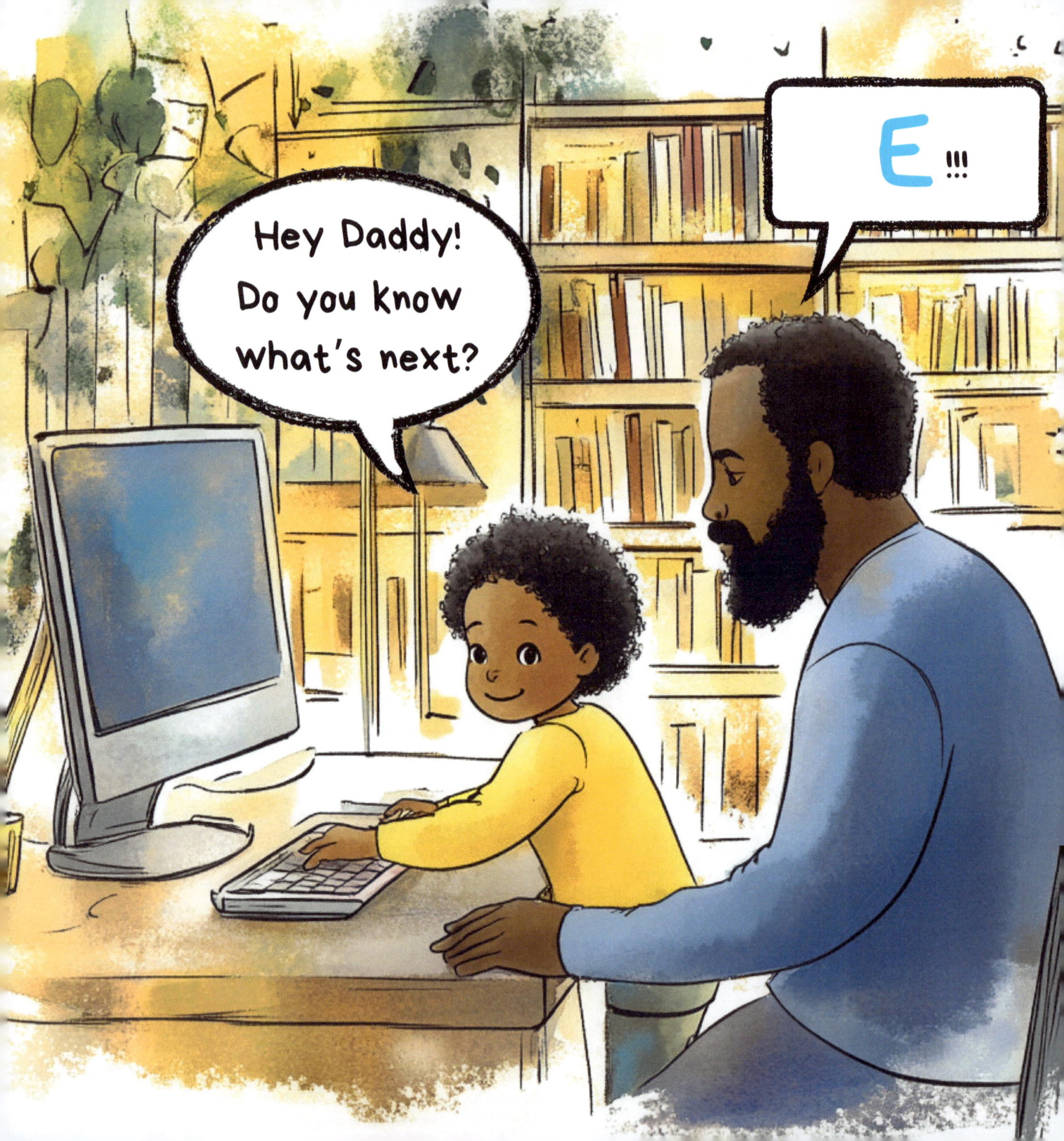
Hey Daddy! Do you know what's next?
E!!!

Alan **E**mtage
created the first search engine.
It's kind of like Google.

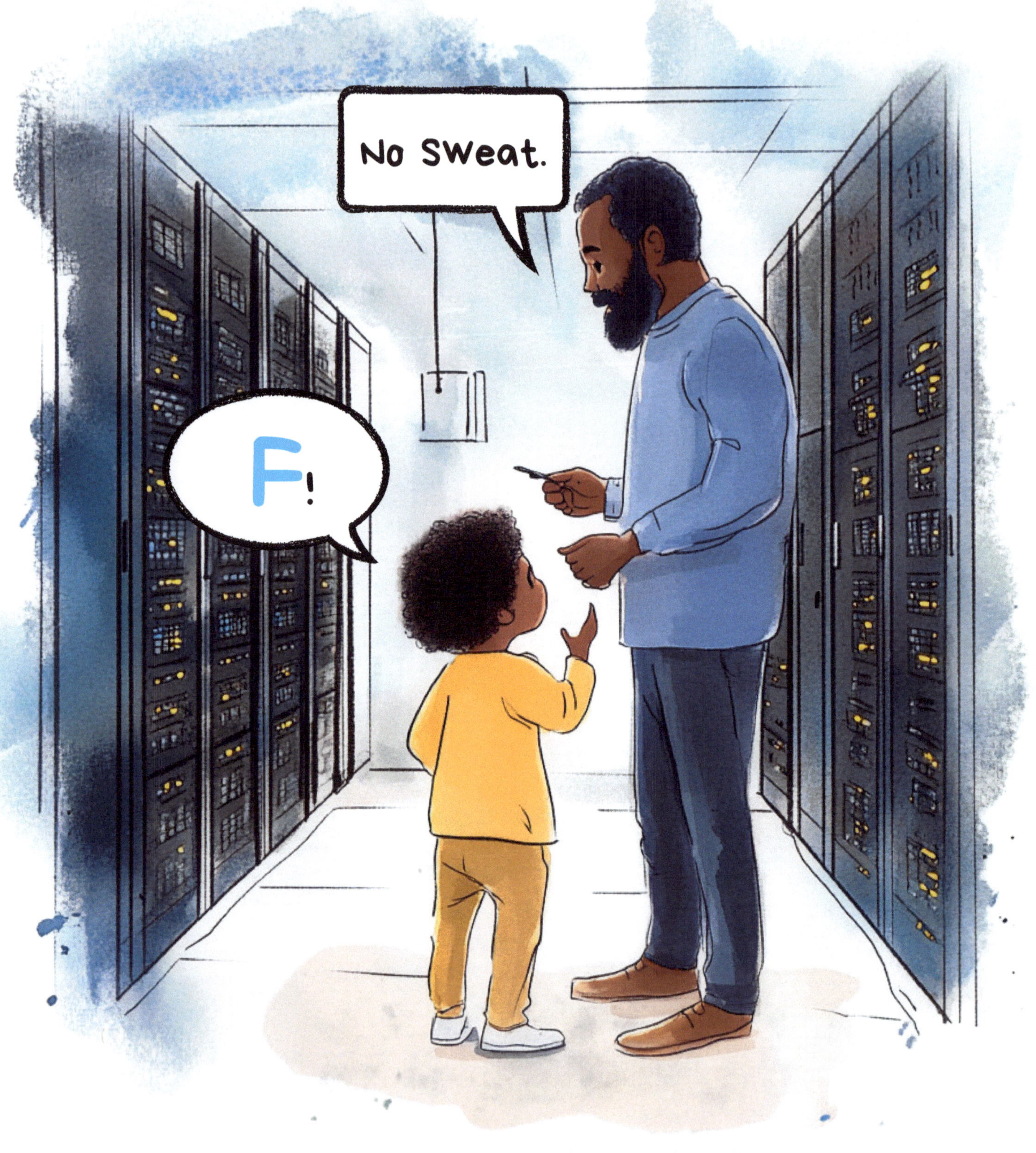
No Sweat.
F!

Brian Fox
made it easier
to tell computers what to do.

Evelyn Boyd Granville
used math to send
people to the moon.

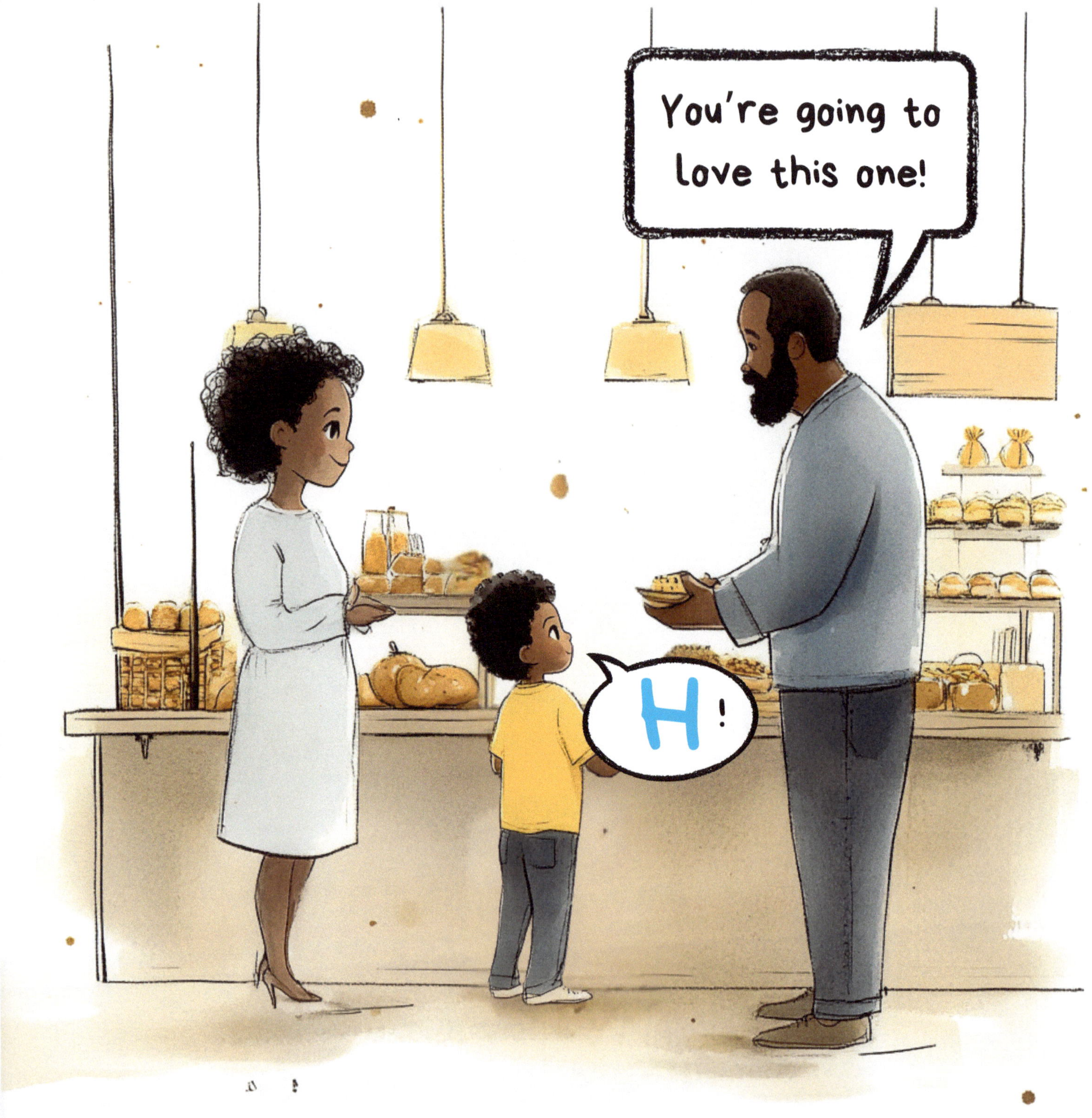
You're going to love this one!
H!

Lloyd Hall
made cookies and cupcakes last longer.

I think this robot spent all his cache.
Hehe. Daddy, what about I?

Dr. Charles Isbell
teaches robots how to help people.

Mae Carol Jemison touched the stars!

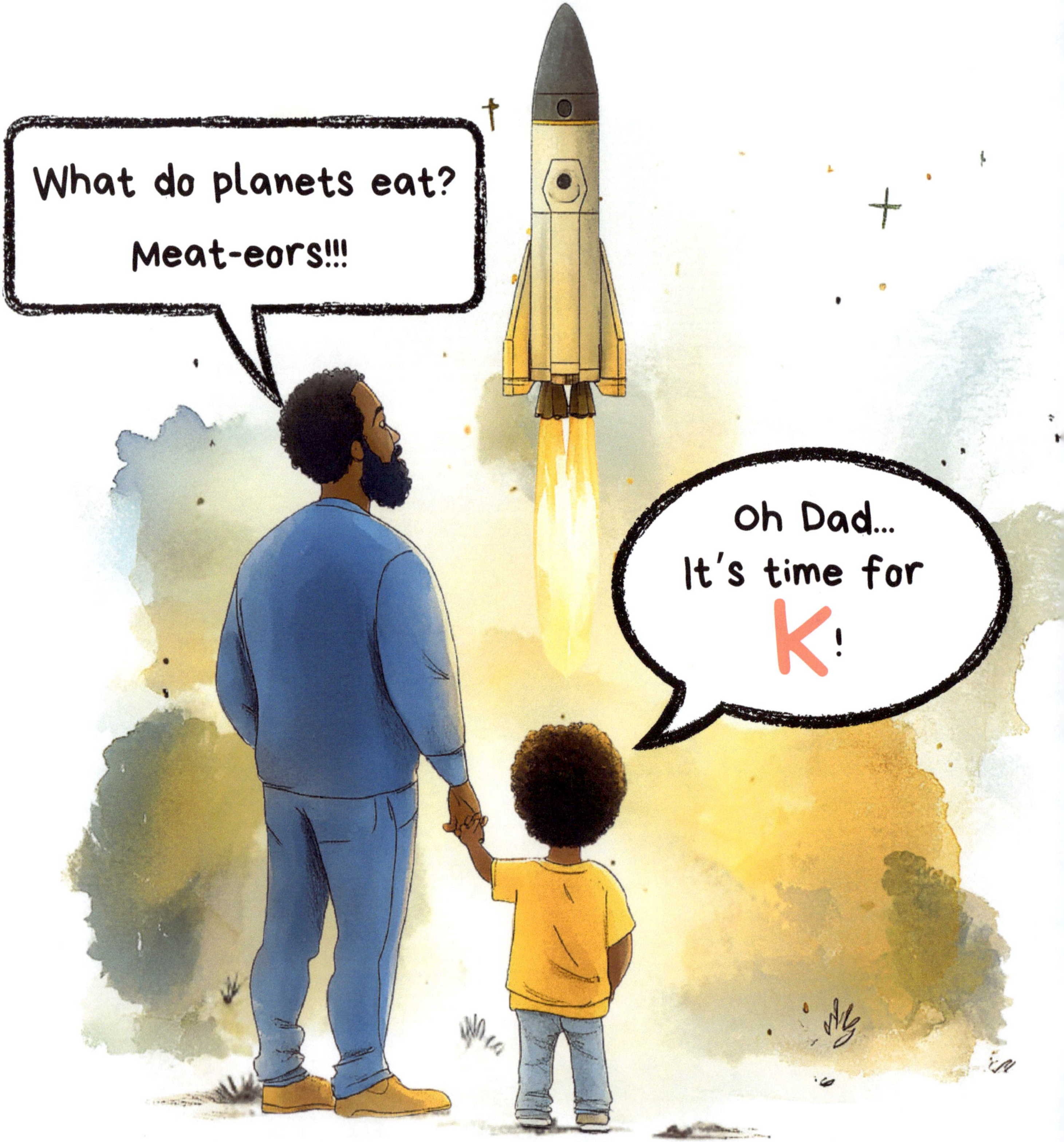
What do planets eat?
Meat-eors!!!
Oh Dad...
It's time for
K!

Katherine Johnson
used math to help NASA send
astronauts safely to space and back.

Jerry Lawson
invented video game cartridges,
changing how we play games forever!

Dr. **M**ark Dean
created a way for us
to plug devices into computers.

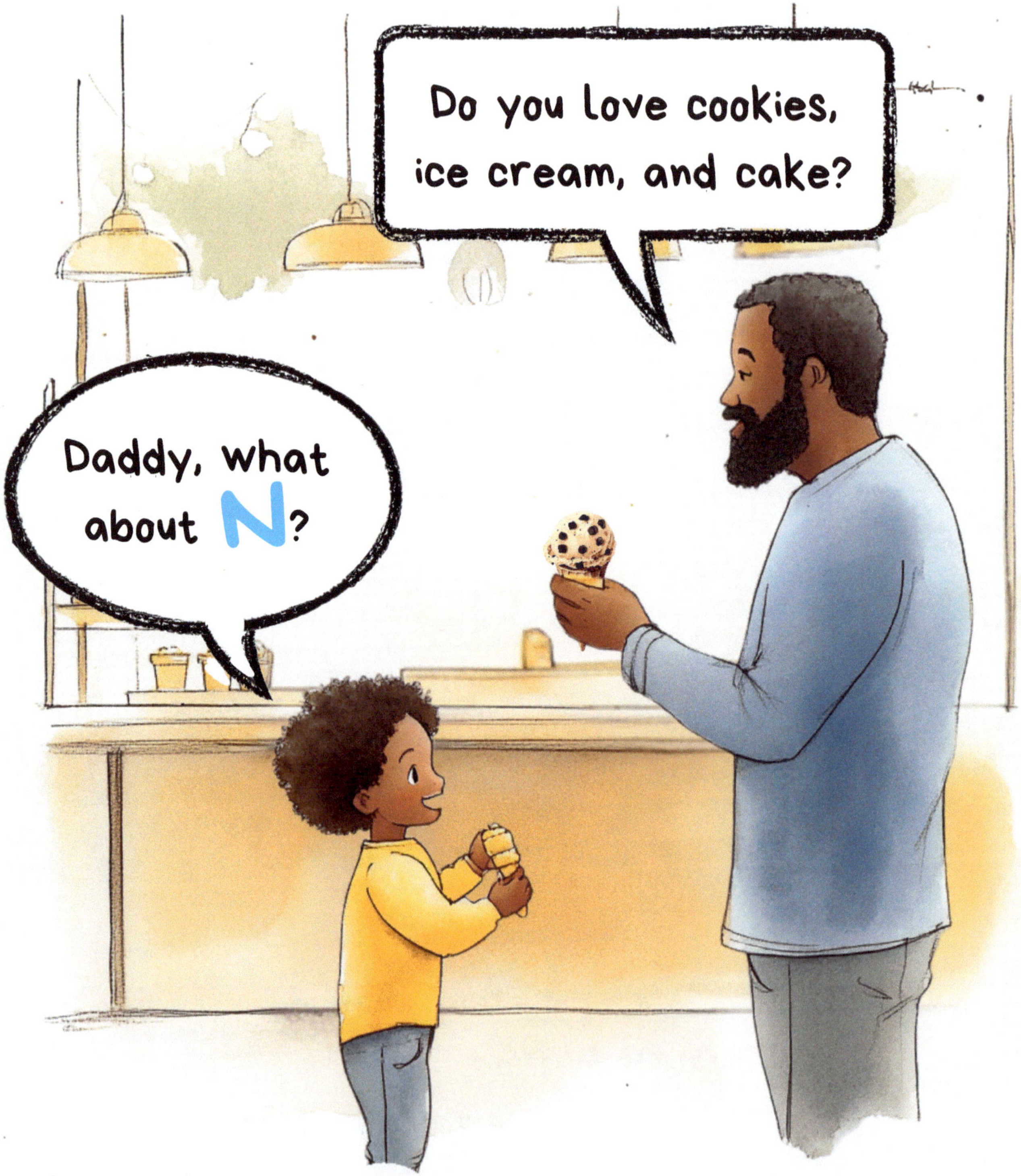
Do you love cookies, ice cream, and cake?
Daddy, what about N?

Well all of them have sugar!
Norbert Rilleux made sugar
easier and safer to make.

Hakeem Oluyesi
studies dark matter to figure out
why our universe is expanding.

Alice H Parker
invented the gas furnace;
it keeps us warm when it's cold.

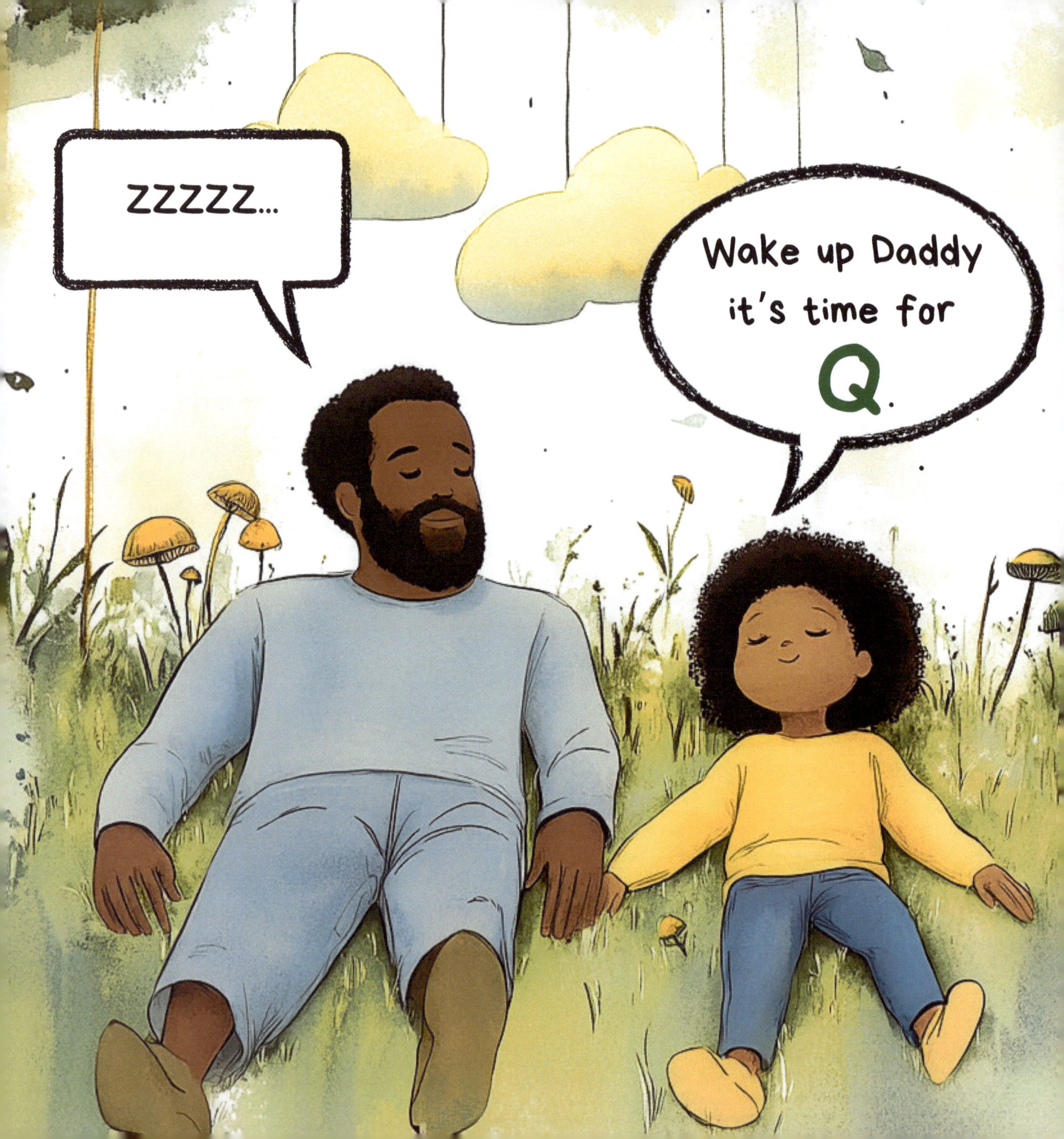
ZZZZZ...
Wake up Daddy it's time for Q.

Lloyd Albert **Q**uarterman
helped create nuclear power.

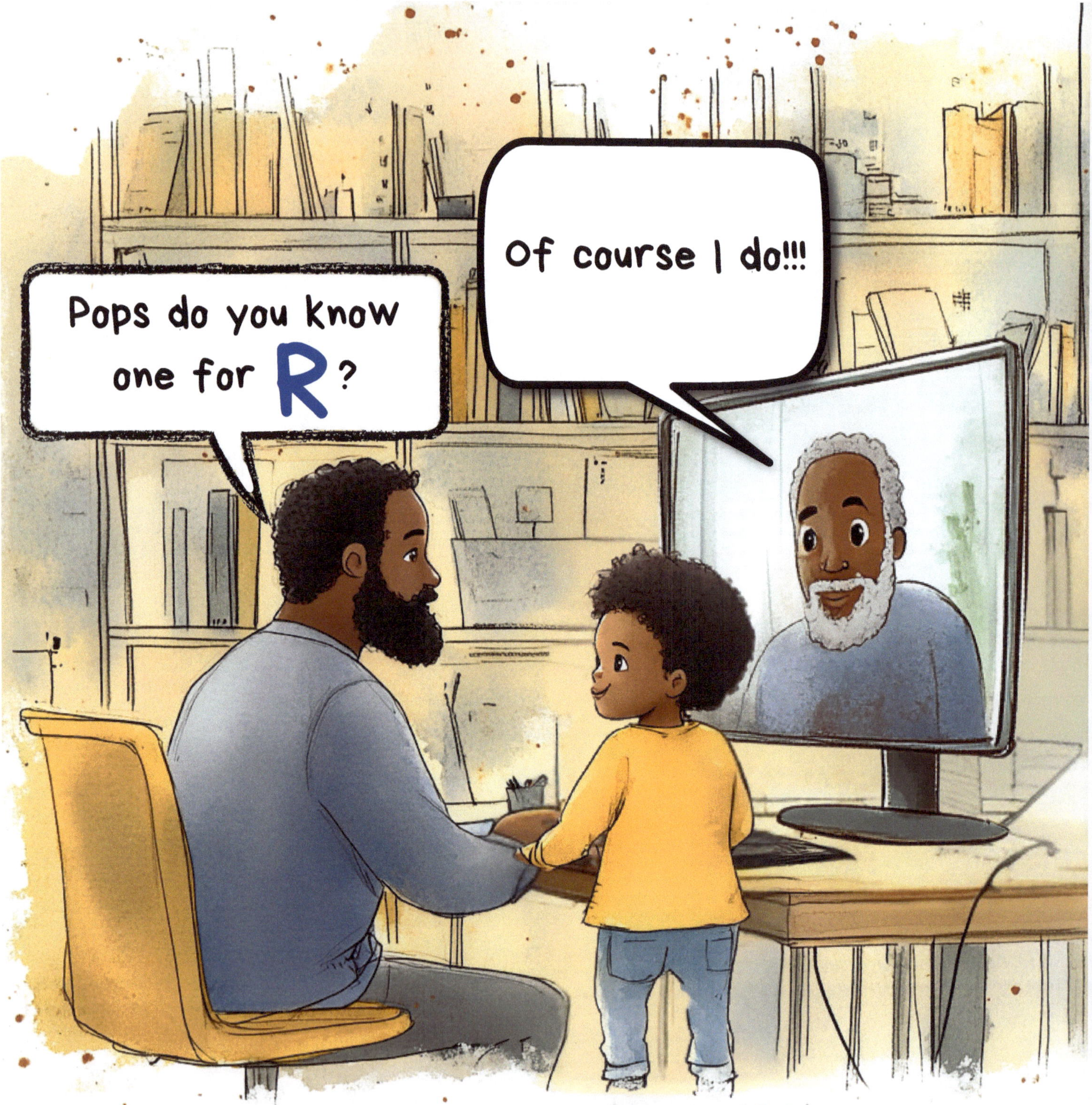
Pops do you know one for R?
Of course I do!!!

Marian **R**ogers Croak
helped us use the internet to talk
to people all over the world.

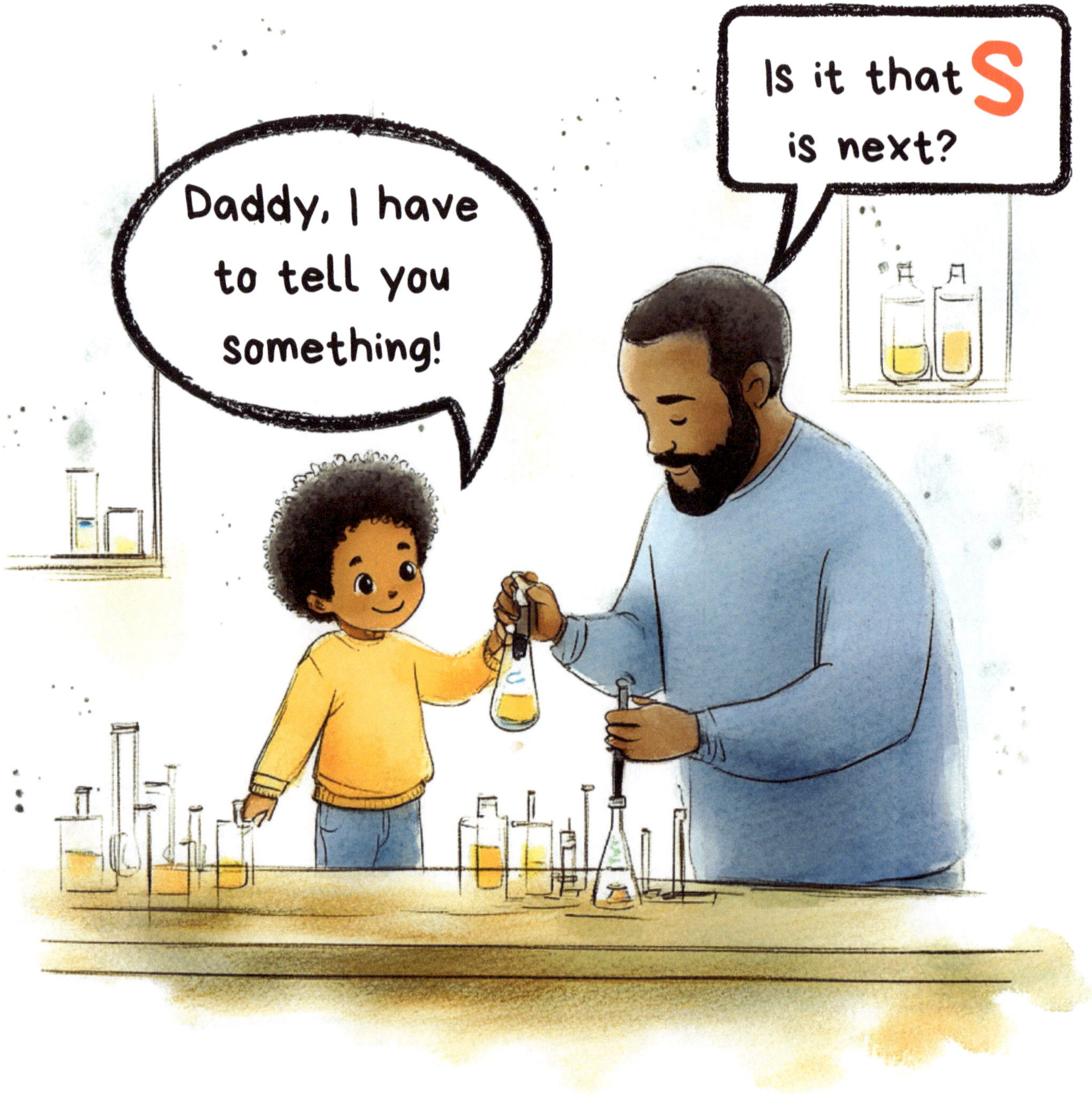
Daddy, I have to tell you something!
Is it that S is next?

Dr. **S**amuel P Massie
saved people by making cures for infections.

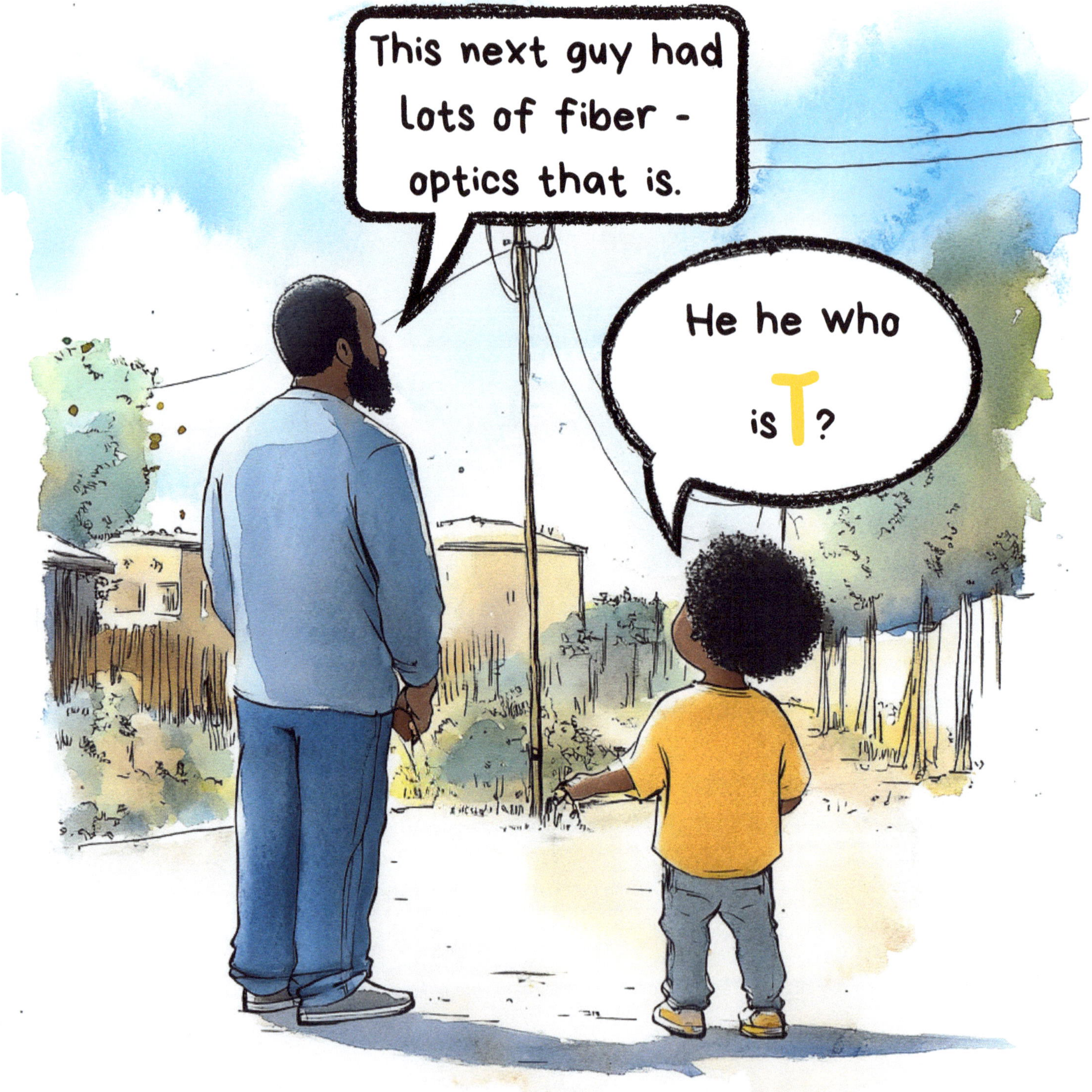
This next guy had lots of fiber - optics that is.
He he who is T?

Dr. Thomas Mensah
made the information on the internet
travel almost as fast as light.

Ursula Burns

went from being an Engineer to running
one of the biggest companies in the World.

Valerie Thomas made a device
that creates 3D images.
It's used in lots of things, like our TV!

Granville T **W**oods
improved many things: the telegram,
telephone, and phonograph.
He even made trains safer.

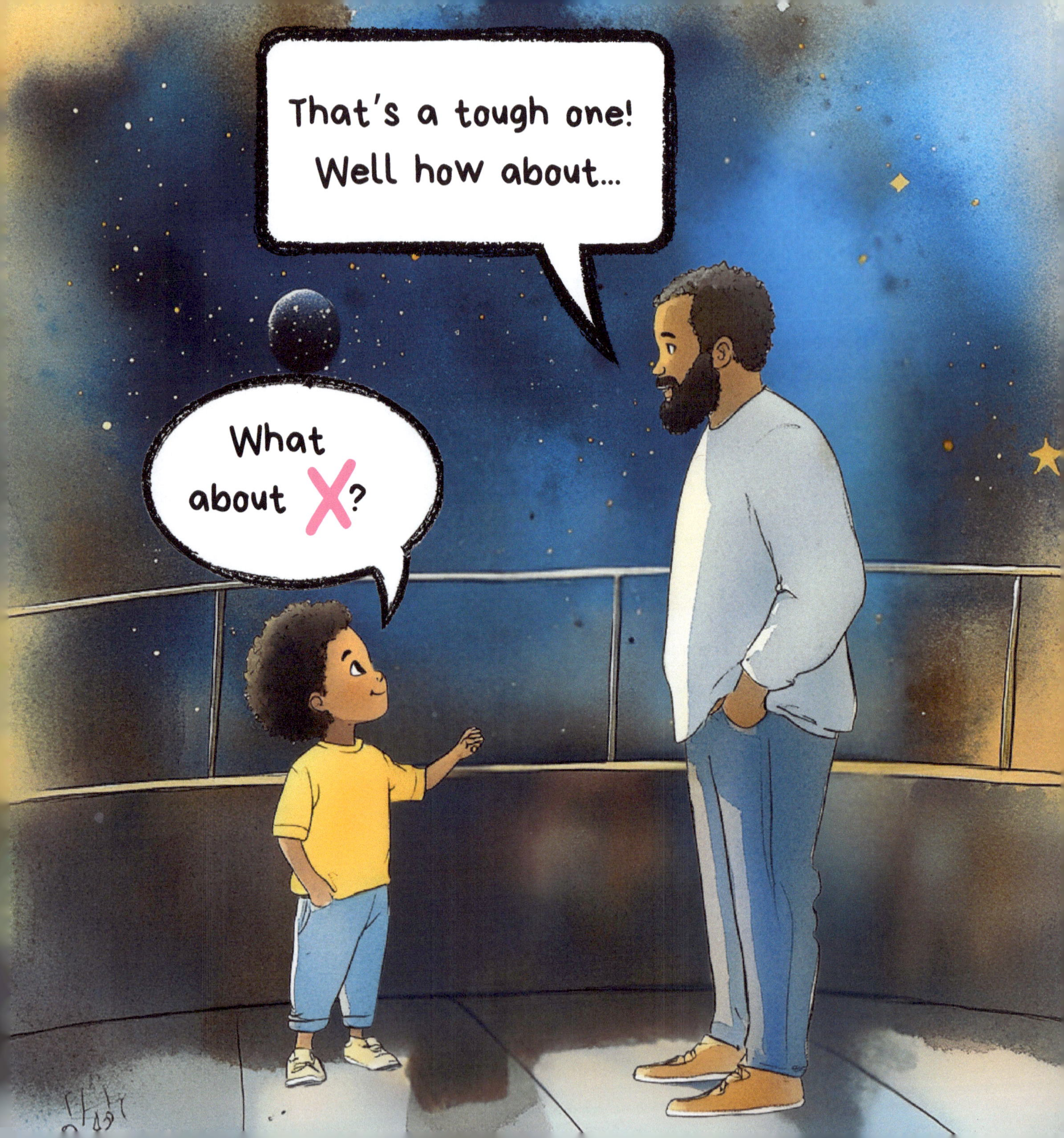
That's a tough one! Well how about...
What about X?

George Edward Alcorn
made an X-ray that can peek
into mysteries from very far away.

Dr. Roger Arliner Young
was a zoologist who studied how
sea creatures live and grow.

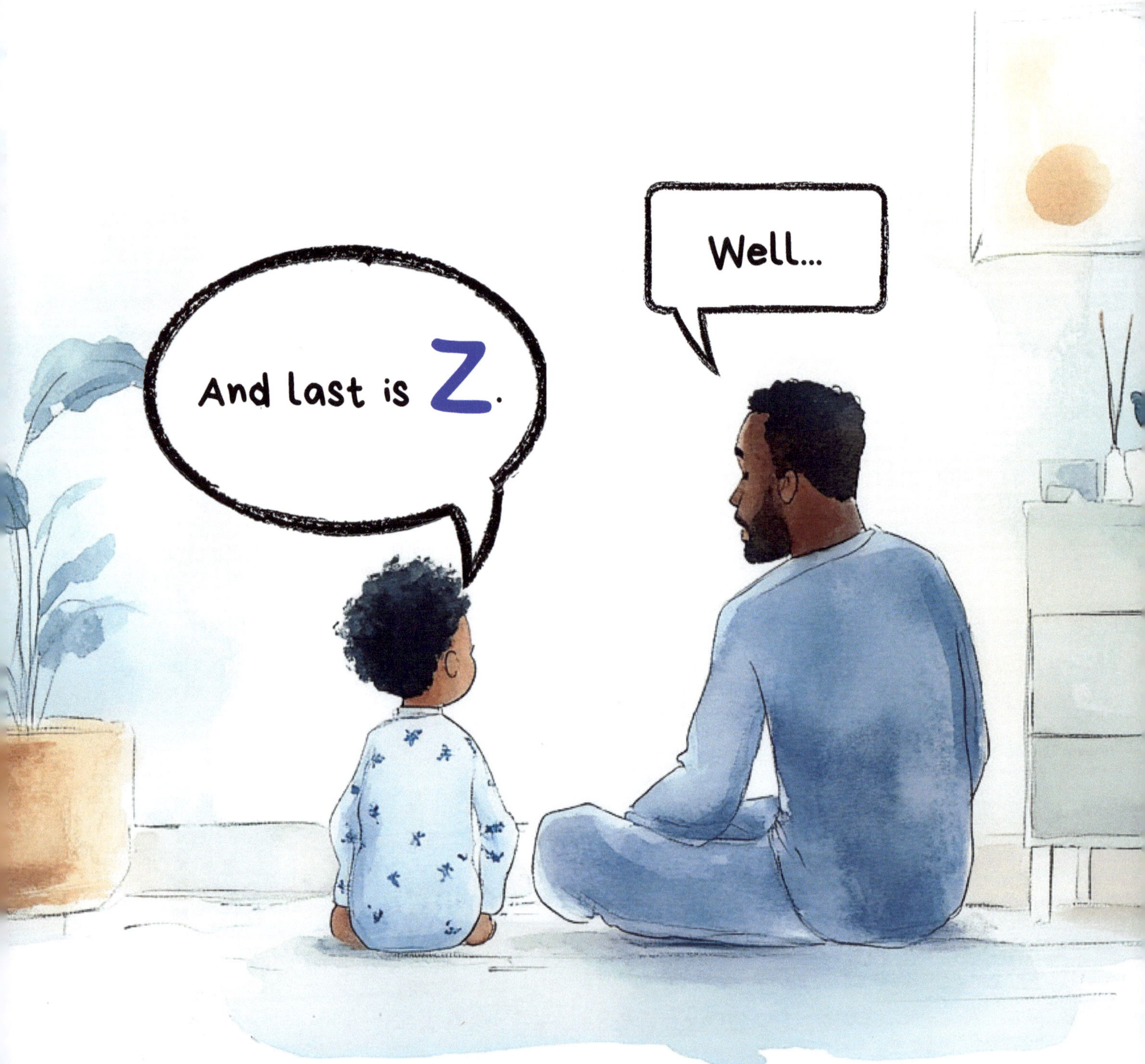
And last is Z.
Well...

Z is for Zulu,
the Maasai, Yoruba, Ashanti, Amhara, Xhosa, Igbo,
and other people that build, dream, and innovate.

www.ingramcontent.com/pod-product-compliance
Lightning Source LLC
Chambersburg PA
CBHW042010080426
42734CB00002B/40